LEEDS

in the Fifties, Sixties and Seventies

LEEDS

in the Fifties, Sixties and Seventies

First published in Great Britain in 2009 by The Breedon Books Publishing Company Limited, Breedon House, 3 The Parker Centre, Derby, DE21 4SZ

All the photographs in this book are available to buy from the *Evening Post's* Photosales website at **www.photostoday.co.uk**

ISBN 978-1-85983-750-4

Printed and bound by Gutenberg Press Ltd, Malta.

Contents

Foreword

The Leeds which so many of us know and love has changed a great deal in the years since the photographs in this book were taken. There are fewer smoke-blackened buildings now, the last tram left the city's streets five decades ago and many traditional occupations, crafts upon which the city's success was built, have long gone. And yet every image reproduced in these pages is clearly of our city. These pictures, taken by Yorkshire Evening Post photographers, reveal a time when Leeds had its feet firmly in its industrial past. Yet there are many which show a city looking forward as well, with the new technology of the time proudly shown off and the skeletons of new buildings rising above the old back-to-back streets.

However, this is not a book about landmark buildings, although there are plenty of pictures of them in here, but rather about the people of Leeds. There are wonderfully evocative pictures of people at work and at play. Many will remember the scenes shown. Some people may even recognise themselves or their loved-ones in the photographs. Look at the pictures more than once. Just as interesting as the characters or buildings in the middle of the pictures are the small details at the edges – street signs, or passers-by, or old cars, or even hair-styles – which take us back in an instant to the Leeds of the fifties, sixties and seventies.

This is a book of wonderful pictures. This is a book of our history. I hope you enjoy it.

Paul Napier
Editor
Yorkshire Evening Post

Introduction

There is an endless fascination about looking at old photographs. They tell us so much about years gone by – not only the buildings and the street scenes, but also the fashions and clothes, all of which gives us an idea of how people lived and how life has changed. This collection of photographs and advertisements is from a comparatively recent era. Most of them are of places and people in the memory of the readers. I hope that they will jog the memory of everyone who is interested in the Leeds as it was in the 1950s, 1960s and 1970s.

One aspect of Leeds is immediately apparent: the buildings in 1950s and 1960s Leeds were black. The accumulation of soot from a couple of hundred years of burning pure coal to power mills and factories, and also to heat homes, left the city's buildings with a distinctive matt black finish. You can still find one or two buildings in the city that keep this blackness, but most of them have now either been demolished or were cleaned in the 1970s. The buildings stopped accumulating their sooty residue after the Clean Air Acts of the 1950s and 1960s, which ended the burning of non-smokeless coal in domestic property. The conversion of mills and new industrial building led to the demise of the mill chimney – it is remarkable how few are left in the city of Leeds.

These photographs show all aspects of life in the city. You will find pictures of tradesmen and workers in the city's industries, office workers, postmen, millworkers – all the workday aspects that make up the city. But mainly you will find buildings. Some of them are buildings that have endured through the ages, and some them were unloved and have been replaced – including the square light-blue Norwich Union building in City Square, which has been replaced by a building that the modern eye finds more appealing. Some buildings in Leeds have been remodelled in recent years, and these photographs show them as they were about 50 years ago.

Many of the streets are instantly recognisable, especially Boar Lane, which has changed remarkably little since the era of trams. There are a few photographs of trams, buses and steam trains, as these methods of transport figure highly in most people's nostalgia for the middle of the last century. Both steam trains and trams almost completely disappeared in Britain in the 1950s and 1960s – although a 21st-century version of the tram may yet return to Leeds's streets.

The pictures show a gentler age, although the city's traffic problems are beginning to emerge. Nowadays it seems almost incredible that in the 1950s those who had cars could drive up and park outside the city's department stores without payment or hindrance. The increasing level of car ownership is reflected in the pictures of the traffic jams in the city in the 1960s, before the 'Loop' road and the one-way system were introduced and the inner relief road became such a vital part of the city's road layout.

1950s

In 1950 the National Book League held an exhibition in the Municipal Buildings on the Headrow. This beautiful room overlooks the Headrow. In the mid-1950s it was altered to house the Commercial and Technical Library. A false floor was inserted, which covered many of the ornate decorative details for decades. This room has now been refurbished and houses a café and shop between the Central Library and the Art Gallery. It is known as the Tiled Hall.

Emigration from the West Indies to Britain started in the early 1950s, and many migrants settled in Leeds. 'A happy Jamaican, Mr G.H. Lewis, who has been in England almost a year and is a bus conductor, typifies the good spirits of the West Indian community in Leeds,' the *Yorkshire Evening Post* reported.

The No. 2 tram to Moortown on Boar Lane in the 1950s. No. 65 was a 1926–27 Brush-Chamberlain, named after the Leeds Tramways general manager William Chamberlain and its makers, the Brush Electrical Engineering Co.

This gas-powered Ford V8 car was owned by Mr J.L. Brown of Leeds, who is seen here loading the furnace in June 1951. It was reported that the performance of the car was poor, and one finished the ride smelling of kippers. The car's fuel was old wooden fences or boxes, but the best was hardwood blocks. Gas-powered cars were used in France during World War Two.

The Odeon cinema on the corner of New Briggate and the Headrow, pictured in 1951. The film being shown is an A certificate, which meant Under-16s were only admitted with an adult. It is almost incredible nowadays that at that time Under-16s would hang around cinemas showing an A film to ask an adult 'Will you take me in please, Mister?'

MAJESTIC AND SCALA LEEDS

GAUMONT THEATRES

Telephone: Majestic 272511 · Scala 270571 STARTS TOMORROW

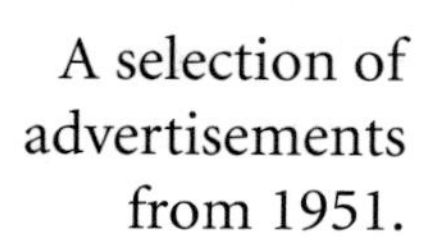
A selection of advertisements from 1951.

A selection of advertisements from 1951.

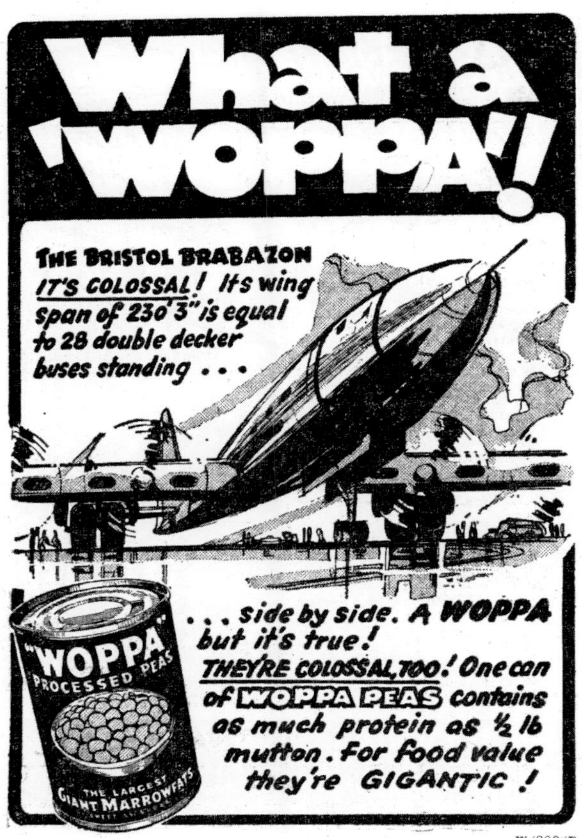

Look to BUSH for Television satisfaction

MODEL TV.22

49 GNS.

(TAX PAID)

Everything in this Bush model TV.22, both seen and unseen, is designed to bring you lasting television satisfaction. The clarity of the picture, the shapeliness of the cabinet, the famous Bush reliability—all of these have been combined at a price which ensures real value for money. Every Bush set is the product of nearly twenty years' experience and skill in the manufacture of television. Ask your Bush dealer to show you the TV.22—you, too, will be enthusiastic when you see what a fine model it is.

BRILLIANT PICTURES
ONLY TWO CONTROLS for normal use.
OPERATES on A.C. or D.C.
SPECIAL CIRCUITS check interference.
SUITABLE TO ANY B.B.C. Television transmitter.

BUSH TELEVISION

BUSH RADIO LTD., POWER ROAD, CHISWICK, W.4

royds T51/11/6

ARMOUR COUNTS-

but men count most!

Britain is building up her armour—and armour, as even King Arthur knew, is a dead loss without a knight inside it! From now on many more men will be needed. Men good enough to hold a position and win promotion in this permanent, highly specialised team of crack combat units—The Regular Army. Have you got what it takes—the brains to master technical weapons, the tough good-humoured character that can learn to obey and command? You have? Then find out what the New Deal for Regular Army men can now offer *you* in pay and prospects. Call today at a recruiting office, or post the coupon below.

There's room for the best today in the

REGULAR ARMY

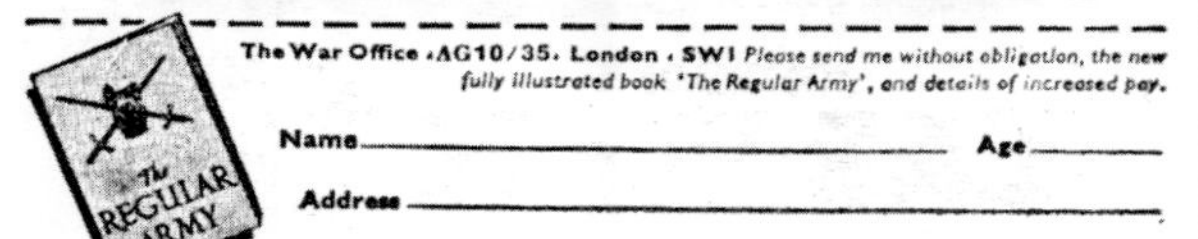

MILLETTS FOR TENTS AND CAMPING EQUIPMENT

SEE OUR SPECIAL WINDOW DISPLAYS!

TWO SPECIAL BARGAINS!

INDIAN ARMY BIVOUAC TENTS
Made from strong Khaki Duck. Complete with poles, pegs, etc. Size 6ft. 6in. long, 5ft. 6in wide. 3ft. high. Packed in small waterproof bag. PRICE (Complete) **52/6**

THE SUFFOLK TENT Made from good quality White Tent Cloth. With jointed poles, guy-lines, pegs etc. Size 7ft. long 6ft wide 5ft. high, 2ft. walls. PACKED IN HANDY BAG **£6-7-6**

Genuine Govt. Surplus SLEEPING BAGS
Outer cover from super quality Cream Cambric, plumply filled and wadded with prime Java Kapok. Made for the troops in Iceland, these are the last word in camping comfort **57/6**
Also SWEDISH PATTERN, with waterproof Outer Cover, with zip fasteners. Lined blanket cloth **59/6**
(Postage and Packing ... 1/6)

150 Brand New R.A.F. DINGHIES
Complete with Inflator & Drogue. Provide hours of fun and pleasure on sea, lake or river (Post 1/-)
79/6

SPECIAL OFFERS IN MEN'S CLOTHING AND FOOTWEAR!

Outsize Men's TROUSERS
In good quality Navy Blue Melton Cloth. Ideal work wear. Waist size 44, 46, 48in. **31/11**
Also MEN'S TWEED TROUSERS with extra long legs. Up to 34in. leg. Post 1/-. **29/8**

250 PAIRS MEN'S GREY FLANNEL TROUSERS
Made from Hardwearing Cloth, in nice medium Grey Shade. Smartly tailored, with belt loops, extension belt, side straps, etc. Post 1/- PER PAIR **23/7**

Another Big GOVT. SURPLUS BARGAIN!
250 PAIRS Naval Tropical Issue Canvas-Top FATIGUE BOOTS
(as illustrated.) Foot upper made from good quality Black Grain Leather. Solid leather soles and heels. Stout canvas leg, 12in. high. Ideal for riders, anglers, farmers, etc. Brand new. Sizes 6 to 11 Post 1/-. **27/6**

Men's Smart HOLIDAY SHOES
With stout canvas uppers, in Brown or White. With thick rubber non-skid soles and heels. Good selection of sizes. For comfort and service. Sizes 6 to 10 Real Bargain at PAIR **18/11**

MILLETTS STORES LTD., 46/47, BOAR LANE, LEEDS 1
TEL. 27119. Please send cash and extra carriage with Post Orders

A selection of advertisements from 1951.

A selection of advertisements from 1952.

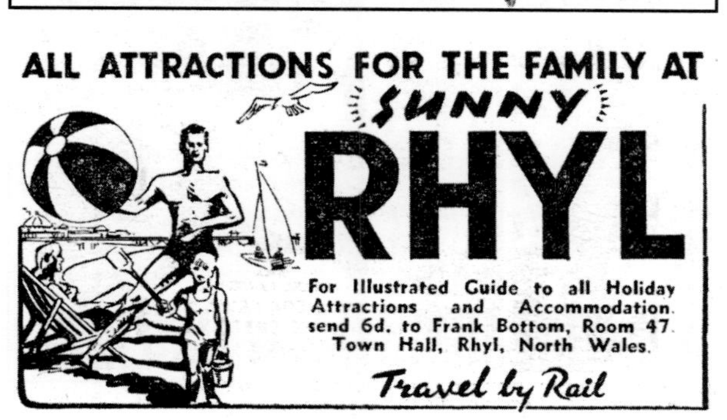

A selection of advertisements from 1952.

WOMEN ARE OVERWORKED

You can see with half an eye nowadays that the daily routine is getting a lot of women down. Not that there's more work—but they seem to lack the energy for what there is . . .

DO YOU FEEL LIKE THIS? Does each task leave you a little more down in the mouth? Are you too fatigued to get through the day properly, without that vitality which makes all the difference?

THERE'S A GREAT HELP Wincarnis can help you back to normal; it's a delicious wine fortified with approved amounts of glycerophosphates beef and malt extracts — a pleasant drink, and so good for you too!

For DEPRESSION · NERVOUSNESS · POOR APPETITE · EXHAUSTION · AFTER ILLNESS

WINCARNIS IS WONDERFUL

A selection of advertisements from 1952.

Leeds, 17 December 1954. An operator at the Leeds GPO plugs into the switchboard and prepares to send a message over the Telex system.

A packed reference library at the Central Library, with tables occupied by readers, in this picture from 1954. This library changed its name to the Business and Research Library, but now this space is occupied by the Local and Family History Library. The Reference Library of Leeds began in 1871 at the Old Infirmary, moving to its present location in 1884.

February 1955: two librarians in the newly opened Law Library in the Town Hall.

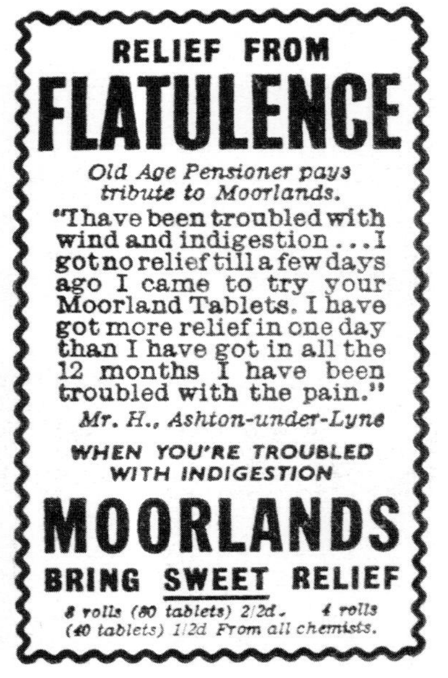

Wednesday 21 September 1955, Flatulence ad.

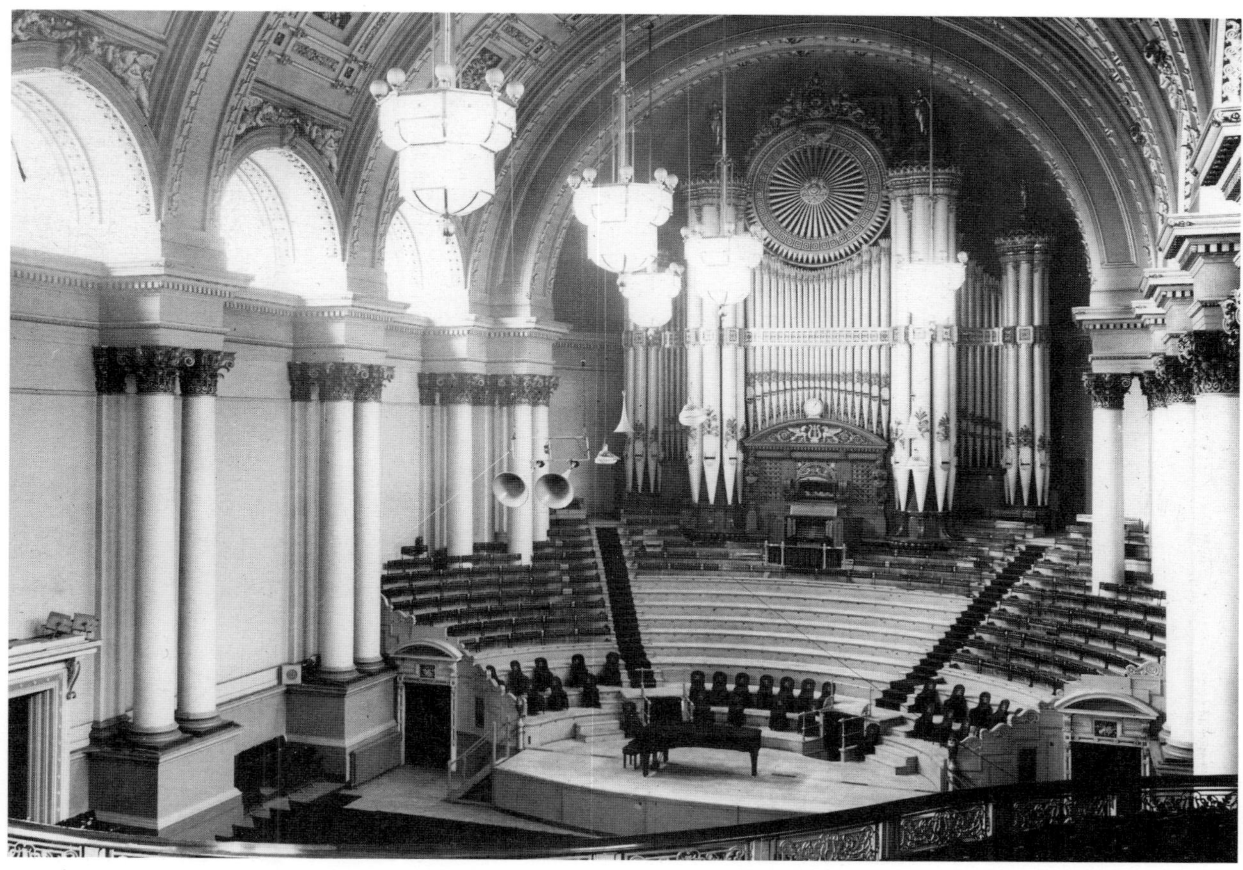

Leeds Town Hall, 1956. This view is from the balcony at the south end of the Victoria Hall.

Close up view of the platform and organ at the north end of the Victoria Hall, Leeds Town Hall, 1956.

Looking from the south entrance of the Victoria Hall, Leeds Town Hall, towards the magnificent organ at the north end, 1956.

The keyboard of the Great Organ situated in the Victoria Hall, Leeds Town Hall, 1956.

A view of the organ installed in Leeds Town Hall, said to be one of the largest in Europe, 1956.

View of the Victoria Hall, designed by Cuthbert Brodrick, looking towards the balcony at the south entrance, 1956.

The view from the stage of the Theatre Royal, Lands Lane, 1956.

Looking up Lands Lane towards Lewis's store on the Headrow in 1956. The Theatre Royal opened in 1826 but was sold to Schofields in 1956 and closed the following year. It was demolished and replaced by Schofields furnishing store. For many people it staged the best pantomime at Christmas in Leeds.

The stage at the Theatre Royal.

Taken in September 1956, this picture shows that the area at the back of the Civic Hall had been cleared. The Civic Hall can seen from the rear. It was designed by E. Vincent Harris and opened by King George V and Queen Mary on 23 August 1933.

City Square alterations, 27 February 1956.

At the Leeds Central Station a Thompson unnamed B1 steam train engine, No. 61164, gets ready to leave in March 1957.

The dense city fogs that affected Leeds city centre in the 1950s almost completely disappeared with the Clean Air Acts, which stopped the use of ordinary coal in domestic property. This picture, taken on 27 November 1958, shows a gas flare in City Square to illuminate the traffic policeman on duty in the fog.

Archway in the grounds of the Teachers' Training College at Beckett Park, 15 October 1958.

15 September 1958: an exhibition in the Art Gallery of French book illustrators of the 20th century. It was organised by René Varin of the French Cultural Service, French Embassy, London.

This photograph shows the last tram to run in Leeds entering the depot after its final journey, on 7 November 1959, to be met by a large crowd of people lining the route. This illuminated tram had come from Cross Gates, Temple Newsam and Halton. Fares varied between 1d and 6d. The first trams in Leeds had run on 16 September 1871 from Boar Lane to Headingley.

McConnell's wine bar in Briggate, March 1959.

In 1959 the Ebor Gardens estate was under construction. This view looks across streets of old back-to-back houses to York Road. The new paths and houses will be part of the Ebor Gardens estate.

Another view of the Ebor Gardens Estate, under construction.

Leeds Head Post Office, 7 December 1959. The final sorting of parcels after they have passed through the Sovex machine.

Leeds Head Post Office, 29 December 1959. The new electronic sorting machine avoids the customary overcrowding and handles mail faster.

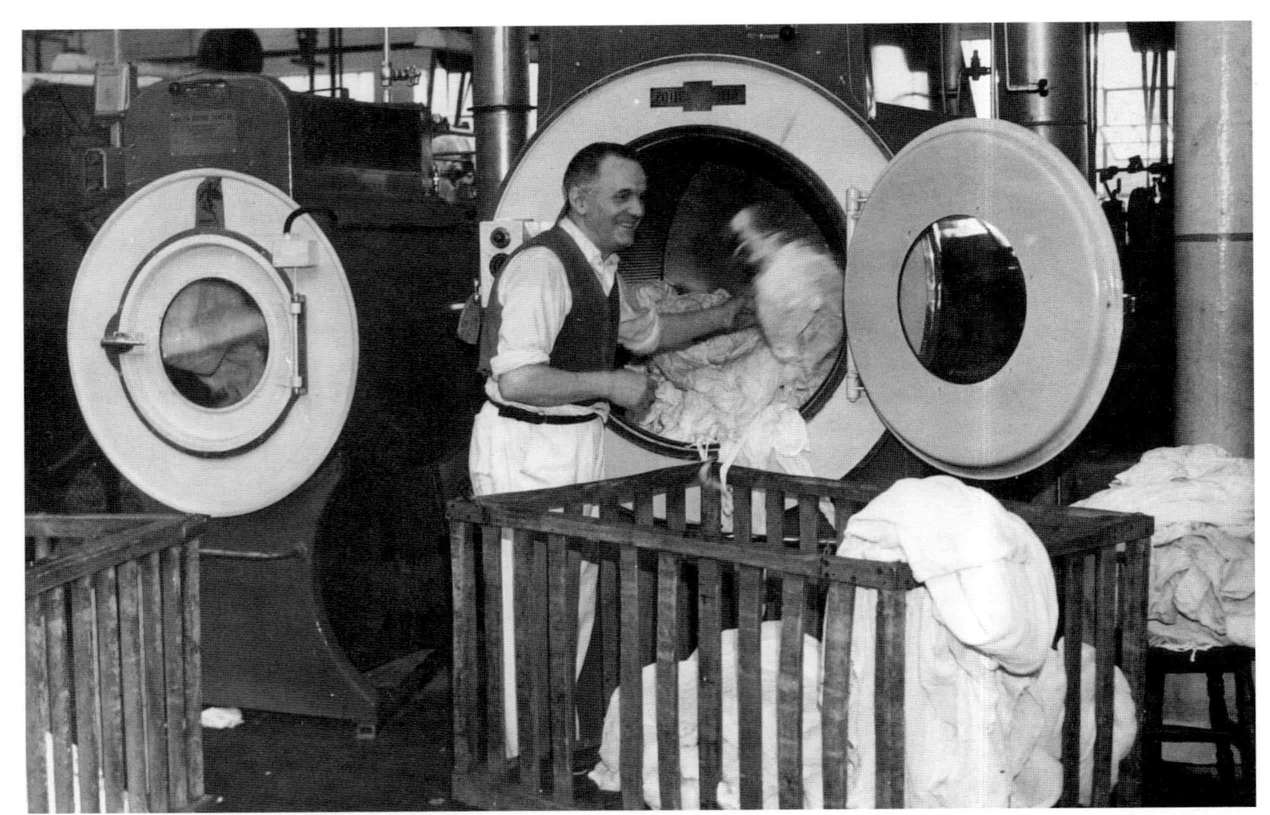

The United Leeds Hospitals Board's new laundry at Whitehall Mills. E. Turner is using one of the large spin dryers, 12 November 1959.

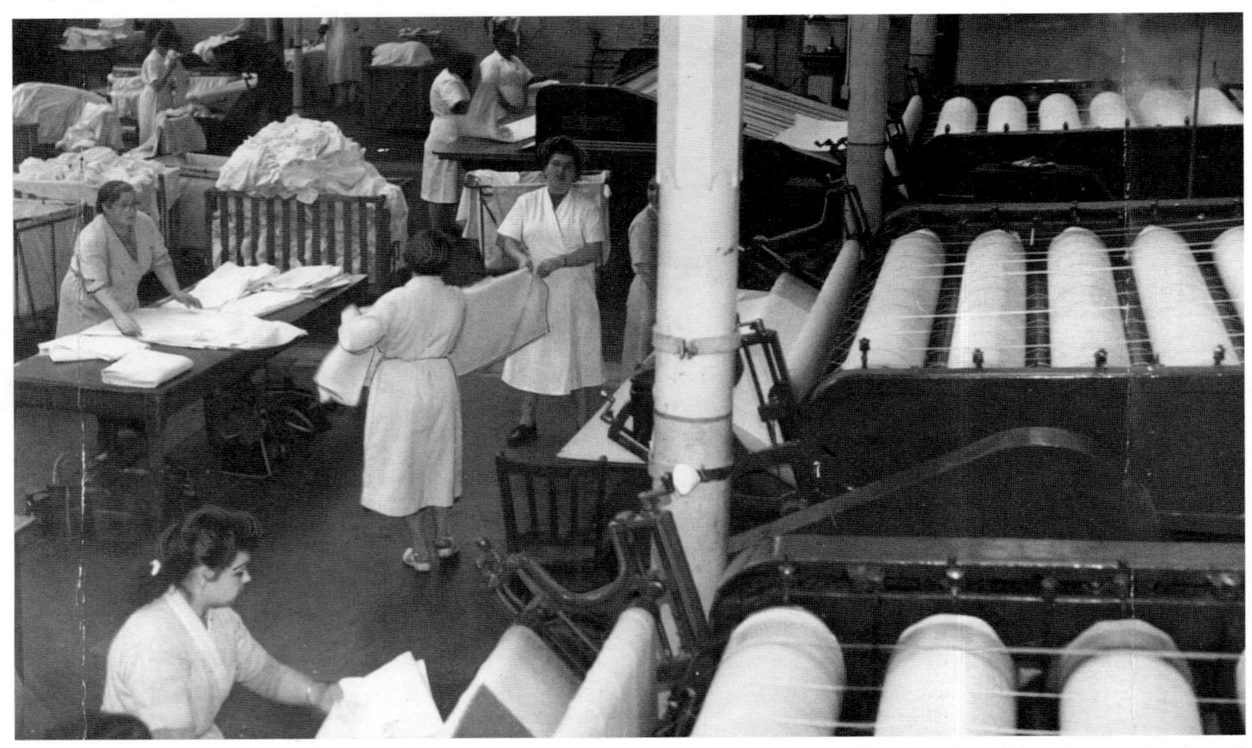

The United Leeds Hospitals Board's new laundry at Whitehall Mills, Leeds. This picture is dated 12 November 1959.

Children admire the illuminated Christmas tree which was placed in the Garden of Rest in the Headrow, 11 December 1959.

1960s

This picture is from the early 1960s, looking from Cross Arcade into County Arcade to the front of the Mecca Locarno Ballroom. This dance hall had opened on 3 November 1938. In 1960 Jimmy Savile, now Sir Jimmy, became manager there. This venue closed in 1969 after a new Mecca had been opened in 1964 in the Merrion Centre.

MECCA LOCARNO
CAFE DANCING

Above and opposite: The County Arcade was designed by Frank Matcham. The cupola was situated in the centre, where the Cross Arcade joined the County Arcade. Constructed between Briggate and Vicar Lane, on the site of White Hart Yard, the arcade is now part of the Victoria Quarter, which was created from the former Queen Victoria Street, roofed in stained glass, and County Arcade.

FURNITURE
EST. 1900

Looking up County Arcade from Vicar Lane to Briggate.

Briggate in the 1960s looking north from Boar Lane. At the bottom left can be seen Saxone Shoes. On the right is Walker & Hall, silversmiths. The street is now one-way (north), but the scene at this corner, minus the traffic, is easily recognisable today.

An artist's impression of the new Odeon Cinema to be built in Leeds during the 1960s.

Leeds Assembly Rooms in the 1960s.

One of the old type of gas lamps in a Leeds street, 21 January 1960.

Leeds telephone exchange, 28 March 1960.

Few of Leeds's skilled tradesmen remain, but this picture from 4 August 1960 shows Mr Ernest Wardman at his cobbler's shop in Cardigan Lane, Headingley.

A policeman on point duty in City Square, Leeds, December 1960.

Civic Hall.

The view across Seacroft from Block One of the Seacroft Gate flats in 1961.

NALGO Jubilee Gardens, 10 August 1961.

This view, in 1961, looks from the top of Seacroft Gate residential flats, Block Two. York Road runs through the centre of the view, with numbers 1000 to 1022 in the foreground to the left. Allotment gardens can be seen behind. Moving back is the Green, then Bailey's Lane and St James's Church. Behind this, Parklands High School and its adjoining playing fields stretch across the view. The cooling towers of Skelton Grange Power Station are visible on the horizon.

From the top of Seacroft Gate Block One in 1961, York Road runs through the centre of this view, with Coal Road joining it from the left. At the junction of these roads are two properties known as Toll-Bar Cottages, referring to the time when York Road was a turnpike. To the right of York Road are four terraced houses which face the camera; these are Pogson's Cottages. Dr William Pogson had been an owner and resident of nearby Seacroft Grange. Behind these properties are houses on Mill Green Gardens.

A cricket match is in progress on the Green, Seacroft, in 1961, with spectators seated on wooden benches. The view is from York Road across the Green to properties including the Cricketers' Arms public house (a large white-rendered building, left of centre). On the right is the old Seacroft Grange County Primary School.

The proposed Leeds market site, 29 June 1962.

These two pictures show Harrison's Almshouses on Wade Lane, one of them with St John's Church in the background. Harrison's Almshouses were the gift of the Leeds merchant John Harrison, who left £1,000 as an endowment. They were originally built in 1653 for 40 poor women, but were rebuilt in 1849. These photographs were taken on 1 February 1962, shortly before their demolition.

The junction of Bond Street and Albion Street in July 1962, with the *Yorkshire Post* Central Advertising Department occupying the corner plot. In 1970 *Yorkshire Post* Newspapers transferred to a new printing and distribution centre in the Bean Ings Mill on Wellington Street.

The new sculpture gallery in the Leeds City Art Gallery was open for visitors on 16 September 1962.

An aerial view of Leeds City Station, 1962.

Mr Roe of Weaver to Wearer, Seacroft, Leeds, 2 October 1963.

Mr Joseph Burgess of South Parkway, Leeds, 12 February 1963.

A knife band cutter is used at the new Seacroft factory by Mr Tom Ginley at Weaver to Wearer, Seacroft, Leeds, 2 October 1963.

View up Eastgate and Headrow late in the evening of 4 November 1963.

View from City House, May 1963.

Reference Library in the Central Library, 1964.

The Hollies, 8 June 1964.

Leeds Corporation public wash house in Kirkstall Road. It cost 3s 6d for two hours washing, 11 June 1964.

The newsroom in Municipal Buildings on the Headrow in 1964. The original newsroom became the entrance to the Art Gallery in 1888. The newsroom was then housed in the new Art Gallery building, then relocated into the library building. Leeds no longer has a dedicated newspaper room.

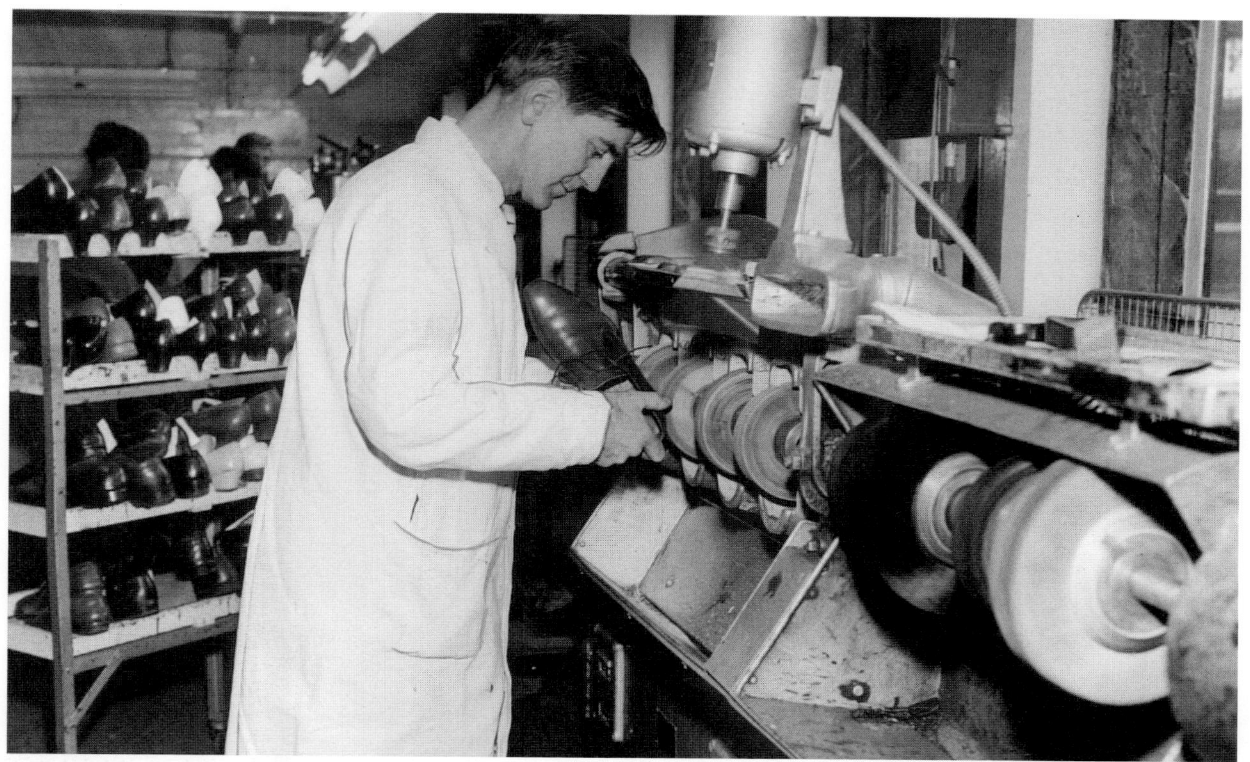

8 October 1964. Cobbling machinery at William Timpson and James Coombes and Co. Ltd. This is the scouring and polishing bench.

The Seacroft Civic Centre was the first large-scale shopping and civic centre development serving a large area on the outskirts of Leeds. This picture was taken on 7 June 1964.

An aerial view of Yeadon, looking north-east, showing Leeds Bradford Airport in September 1964. A new 5,400ft runway, running from left to right in the picture, had recently been constructed, crossing the old runways.

Another aerial view of Leeds Bradford Airport, this time looking north-west, again in September 1964, showing the new 5,400ft runway through the centre from top to bottom, crossing the two existing runways. The central tower and terminal buildings are at the top centre of the picture, and on the top right is the site of the Avro factory, which built bombers during World War Two. Yeadon Tarn is top left, with Horsforth golf course and a reservoir.

Caressa House on King Street was the Leeds headquarters of Wilkinson Warburton, the Yorkshire clothing business which can trace its roots back to 1834. The red neon nymph was considered quite 'racy' for Leeds, but was a landmark on Wellington Street. This picture was taken on 4 December 1964.

City House above Leeds City station, which was being considered as the headquarters of the new Yorkshire Regional Development body. The picture is dated 16 June 1964.

This picture, taken on 17 February 1965, was taken at Leeds-Bradford Airport, and the new extended runway at the airport was due to be completed in three weeks. It was too late for this British Midland Aviation Douglas DC3 Dakota, which overshot the runway and ended up in the workings for the runway extension. The passengers suffered only cuts and minor bruises. The flight was from Derby to Glasgow via Leeds.

The development of Leeds-Bradford airport in the 1960s. These three photographs show the airport apron crowded with planes on 4 June 1965 (top); work in progress (bottom); and the completed terminal on 30 May 1968 (middle).

Dressed in provisional uniform are Leeds's first three women parking meter attendants, who officially started work on 21 June 1965 in Kirkgate, Leeds. Comparing notes are (left to right): Mrs Barbara Smith of Meanwood, Mrs Maureen Rush of Harehills and Mrs Pat Roberts of Armley.

The new offices of the Eagle Star Insurance Company on the Headrow, 24 June 1965.

Albion Street, 8 November 1965. Two office girls arrive with the post at the overworked pillar box in Albion Street, Leeds.

In 1965 the new library at Belle Isle was opened.

Hunslet Cemetery, 1965.

Senior meter attendant J. Burgin standing near one of the Leeds parking meters 25 March 1965.

A policeman on traffic duty in City Square, 1965.

A selection of advertisements from 1965.

NOW SHOWING AT THE

ODEON LEEDS 30031 THE HEADROW

20th CENTURY-FOX Presents

FRANK SINATRA
AND
TREVOR HOWARD

INTRODUCING RAFFAELLA CARRA

COLOUR BY DE LUXE

Co-starring BRAD DEXTER · SERGIO FANTONI
JOHN LEYTON · EDWARD MULHARE · WOLFGANG PREISS

Produced by Directed by Screenplay by
SAUL DAVID · MARK ROBSON · WENDELL MAYES and JOSEPH LANDON

Based on the Best Selling Novel by DAVID WESTHEIMER. A P-R Productions Picture

A selection of advertisements from 1965.

These two photographs taken in 1966 show the old Bank of England building on South Parade and at the corner of Park Row. This view looks from the end of Cookridge Street across the Headrow to Park Row. The bank building has a Greek key design above the first floor windows, and the architect was Philip Hardwick. It is now a bar and nightclub.

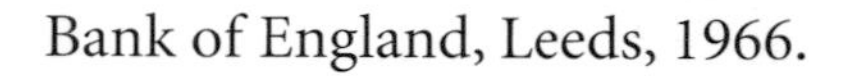

Bank of England, Leeds, 1966.

It is 10 December 1966 and Briggate is as busy as ever in December in the run-up to Christmas.

This picture of Gibraltar Barracks in Claypit Lane, at the junction with Grove House Lane, was taken in 1966, just before their demolition. The barracks was the base of the Royal Corps of Signals, 49th (West Yorkshire) Divisional Signals.

A sealed glass jar was found in the rubble of the demolished building containing relics that had been buried in the foundation of the 1889 extension. They included a copy of the building plan, designed by architect William Bakewell.

The Salvation Army hostel in Lisbon Street at the end of Wellington Street, pictured in August 1966.

The Nag's Head pub in Chapel Allerton dates back to 1772, and according to local legend the original innkeepers were in league with 18th-century highwaymen.

Kissing couple, 22 June 1966.

Archway in the grounds of the Teacher Training College at Beckett Park, 17 October 1966.

Burley Library's display for National Book Week, 1966.

Part of a display for National Book Week, showing Ladybird books, 1966.

Burley Library's National Book Week display, 1966.

Children looking at a display for National Book Week in Burley Library, 1966.

Scholes, near Leeds. It is 25 November 1966, and this picture is of the new St Philip's Church at Scholes, which was to be to be consecrated by the Bishop of Ripon on 27 November 1966.

Two new Sunbeam Tiger GT cars were delivered to Leeds City Police in 1966 and were used by the traffic department. The picture is dated 22 July 1966.

Corn Exchange, 1966.

8
7
G.&J. NICKSON
& CO. LTD.
HEAD OFFICE

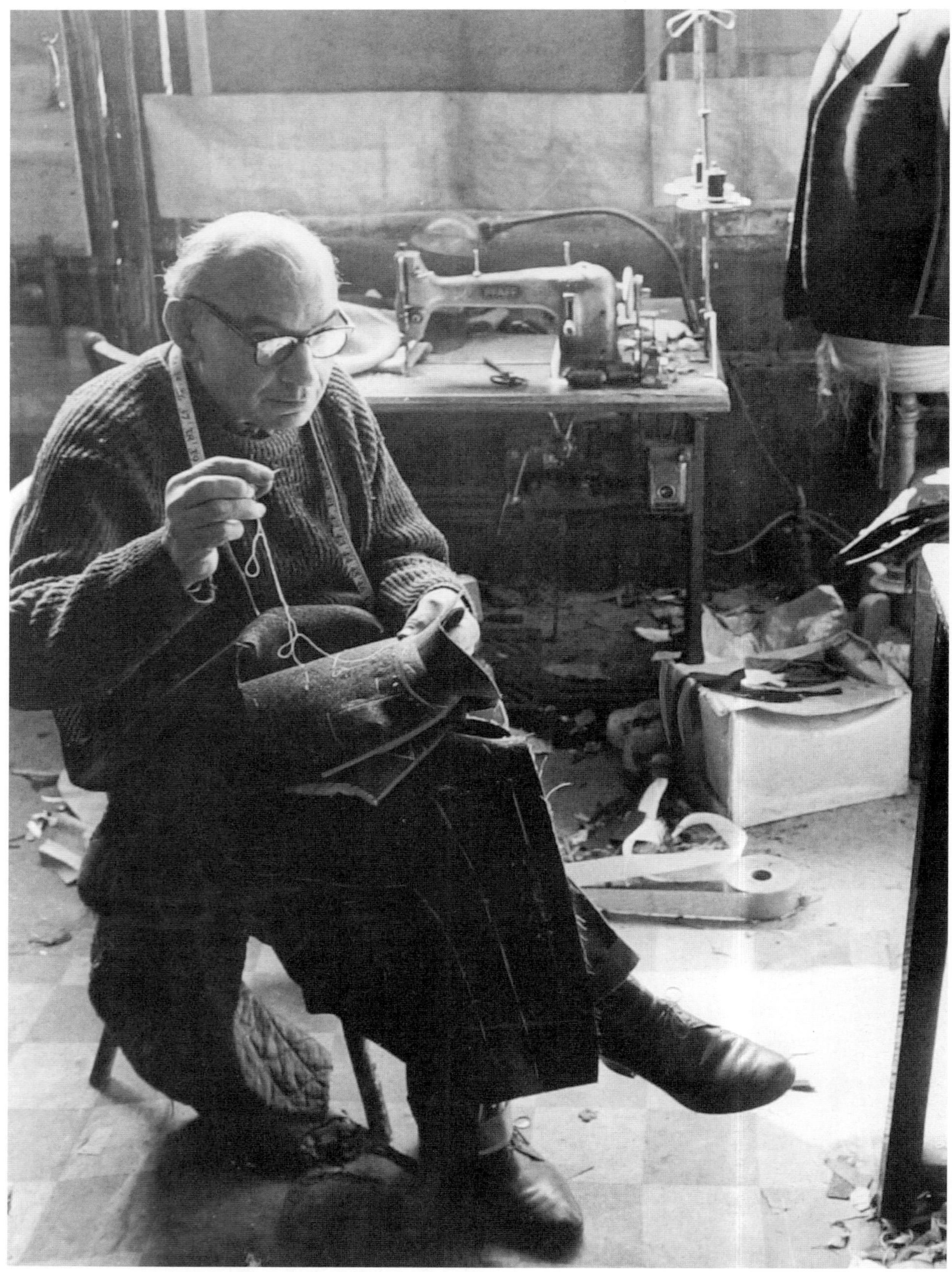

Mr H. Lawrence, of Wintoun Street, Leeds, 3 October 1966.

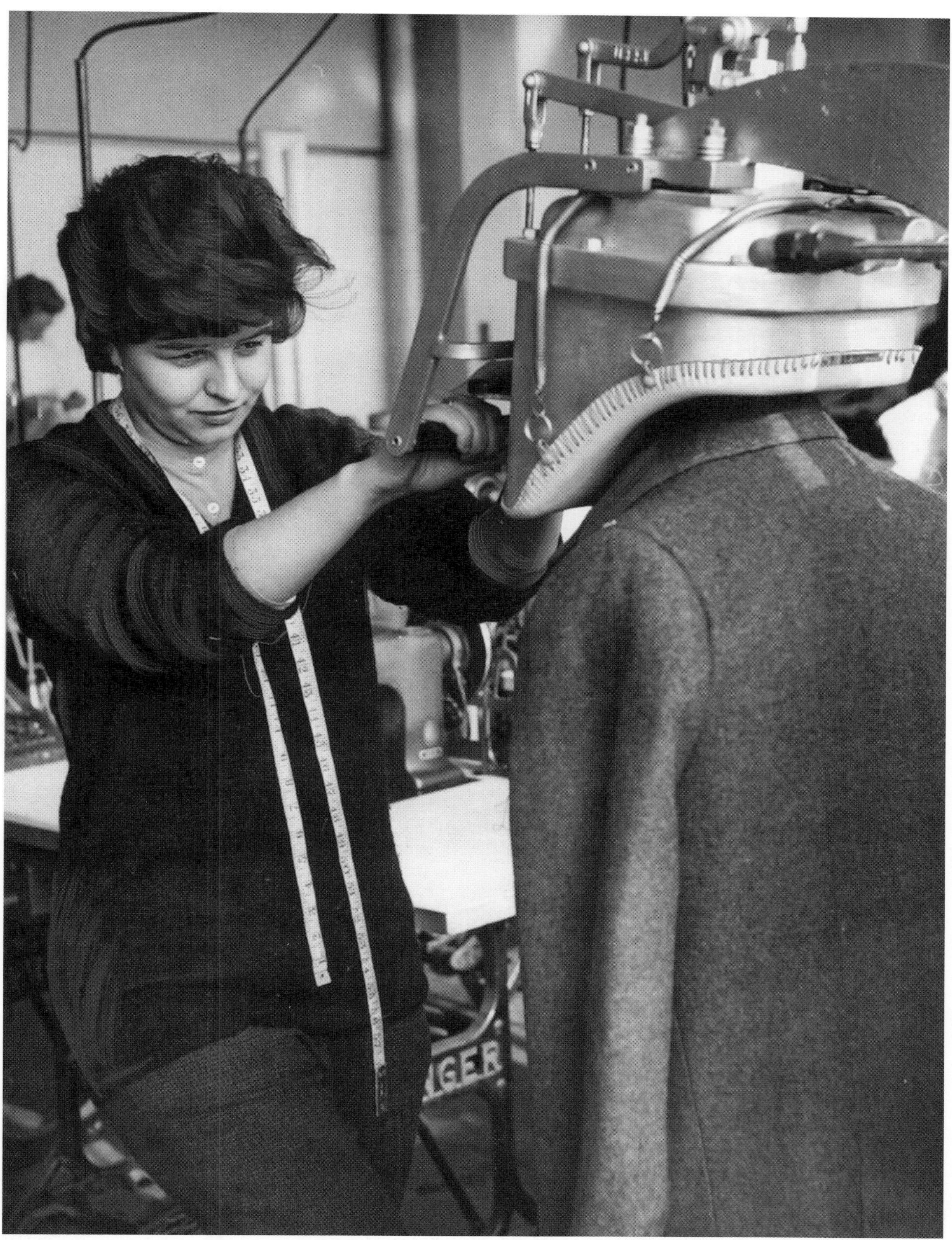

Leeds College of Technology Clothing Department, 21 March 1966. Vanessa Cluley, a full-time student, is at work with a Collarmaster Press in the process machine room.

Clerical Medical Assurance House, 30 November 1966.

The new look Leeds City Police car, 23 September 1966. It has an illuminated sign on top and large letters on each side.

The November gloom over Leeds in 1966. The picture was taken from the top of the new multi-storey block at Leeds Central Colleges.

The three Leeds women traffic wardens who started work in the city on 22 April 1967. Left to right: Mrs Irene Miller, Mrs Marjorie Clark and Mrs Violet Johnson. They are pictured with Police Sgt Norman Hardy.

Upper Basinghall Street telephone exchange, 3 November 1967.

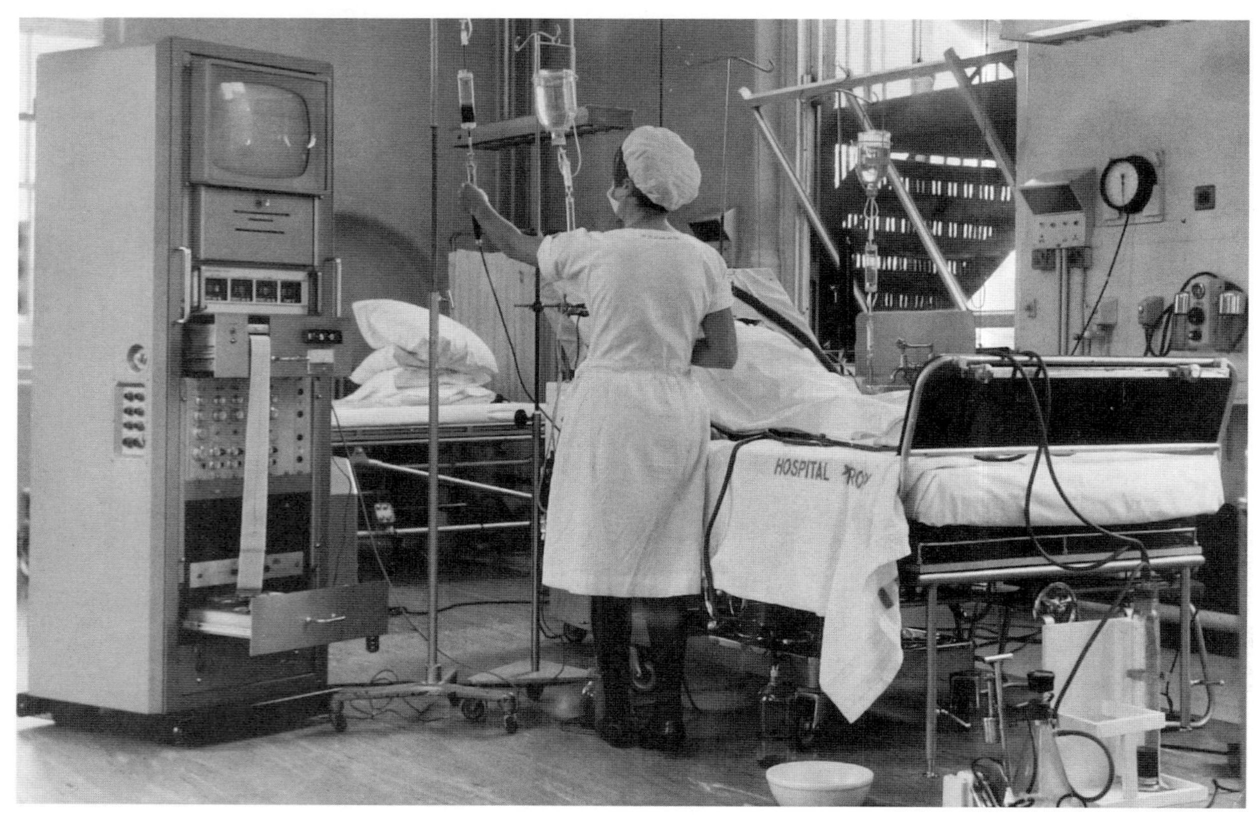

Intensive care unit, Leeds General Infirmary, 1967.

St James's Hospital, 1962. Dr R.M. Holman vaccinates Sister D. Bradley against smallpox. Staff in Leeds hospitals were vaccinated as a precautionary measure.

The Odeon cinema on the corner of New Briggate and the Headrow, August 1967.

The Guardian Assurance Building, 1 May 1967.

Mrs Sandra Rowan and her two-year-old son, Jason, shopping in Leeds, 20 November 1967.

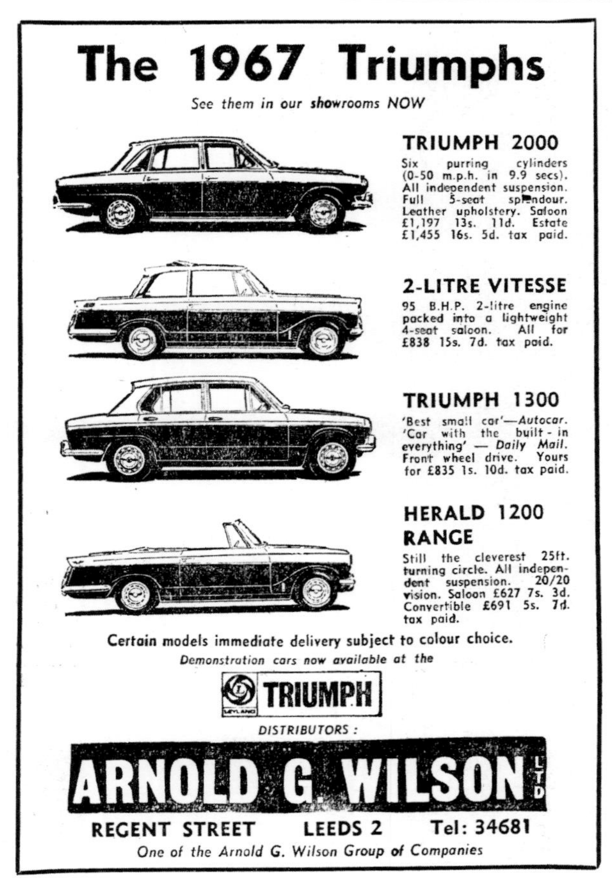

A selection of advertisements from 1967.

A selection of advertisements from 1967.

Rent clean work garments like these for as little as 2/6 a week!

Spring Grove's unique economy rental plan means:—

* No capital outlay
* Individually measured garments
* Free delivery and collection
* Free processing
* Free repair and replacement

Spring Grove reliability means trouble-free service for you, week in and week out. You pay only a small weekly rental charge — nothing else!

A selection of advertisements from 1967.

What is a Luncheon Voucher really worth?

Don't take it at its face value. The intrinsic worth of the Luncheon Voucher Scheme is something no responsible employer can afford to overlook. And the employer who gives Luncheon Vouchers is investing only a little for a very big return. This is a Welfare Scheme that provides an incentive to both existing and prospective staff–*any* staff–from shop workers to executives. It ensures them a mid-day meal–and their vouchers cost them nothing. Even just 3/- a day helps towards paying for lunch. And over 13,000 restaurants in the British Isles accept Luncheon Vouchers. The benefits to the employer are many–nearly 19,000 employers, large and small, have discovered this fact. These benefits are given in detail in the Luncheon Vouchers brochure. They are all worth considering.

Just a note on your business letterheading will bring you this brochure.
A few moments well spent

LUNCHEON VOUCHERS LTD

Northern Area Sales Office:
Castle Chambers, Castle St. Liverpool 2. Tel: Maritime 2541/2
Head Office: 22 Golden Square, London W1 Telephone: REGent 5711/0693

LEEDS' NEW TOUCH TYPING CENTRE (where you learn to touch type in only 12 hours) has a vacancy for ANOTHER MEMBER OF STAFF

If You are a Copy Typist

you could have the qualifications for this unusual and interesting post.

The work will be to assist in the organisation and running of the new Sight and Sound Education Centre (you will not be a teacher - machines do this) but you will need a helpful disposition and a pleasant and confident personality with a touch typing skill. Age should be between 23 and 35.

Hours are from 12 until 7 p.m. Monday to Friday and the salary will range between £600 and £700 per annum.

Write in confidence to Mrs. K.M.Senior, Sight and Sound Education, C/o Personnel Officer, Yorkshire Evening Post, Albion Street, Leeds 1.

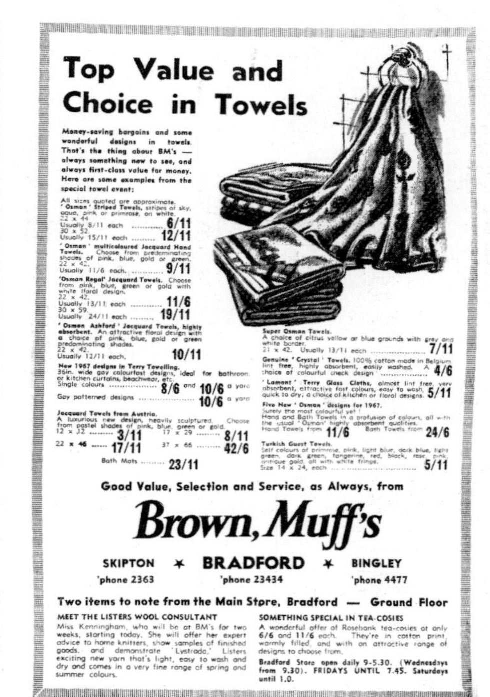

This aerial view of Brotherton House on the lower Headrow was taken in 1967 and looks from Westgate across the City Centre. The Headrow is on the left, with St Paul's Street to the right. In the centre at the junction is Brotherton House, the former offices of a chemical manufacturing company which was purchased by Leeds City Council in 1963. It provided a new headquarters for Leeds City Police in 1965 until 1976 when a new headquarters was opened at Millgarth. It is still occupied by West Yorkshire Police.

This aerial view shows Westgate and the new Inner Ring Road in 1967.

A photograph of Leeds Civic Hall taken in March 1967 from the roof of Leeds Town Hall. The Brotherton wing of the General Infirmary is on the left. Both buildings show the blackness that was a feature of Leeds buildings until the 1970s.

Thirty former Lord Mayors and Lady Mayoresses of Leeds were invited to Leeds Civic Hall on 6 November 1967. They had held office over the previous 35 years.

Lawrence Wilson & Co. at Guiseley, near Leeds, are best known as the makers of Silver Cross prams. This picture, dated 17 June 1967, was taken in the heavy press shop.

The newly built Assembly Hall in 1967, part of Leeds Grammar School on Moorland Road. The school moved to Alwoodley in 1997, and this building was demolished when the site became part of Leeds University.

The Norwich Union building under construction at No. 1 City Square in 1968. This square building, unkindly called the ugliest in Leeds by readers of the *Yorkshire Evening Post*, was demolished in 1995 to be replaced by the new curved Norwich Union Building. Behind is a still uncleaned dome of Leeds Town Hall, and to the right is the edge of Mill Hill Chapel, built in 1848.

Bishopgate Street on 17 May 1968. Looking from City House towards City Square with the old Norwich Union Building.

The old bear pit on Cardigan Road in 1968. It opened in 1840 for the Leeds Zoological and Botanical Gardens, but closed in 1858.

This photo, taken on 20 August 1968, shows the newly opened coin-operated laundry at Harrogate Road, Moortown.

In 1968 Holborn Towers, a multi-storey block of flats off Woodhouse Street, Leeds, contrasts with the cobbled street, the terrace houses and the lines of washing. Holborn Towers, standing 150ft high, was built in 1965 and has 17 floors.

Leeds City Varieties in 1968. The much-loved Leeds City Varieties started from a singing room in the White Swan coaching inn, built in 1762 on this site. Charles Thornton rebuilt a singing room over a newer White Swan Inn, which was opened as Thornton's new music hall in 1865. The tradition of variety theatre was upheld by the world-famous *Good Old Days,* which ran for 30 years on television.

This picture shows County Arcade before its transformation into the Victoria Quarter shopping centre. It was taken in 1968.

Hunslet Grange Flats, nearly always known as Leek Street flats, in 1968. These were built to replace the old back-to-back terraces, which were demolished for slum clearance. There were 2,500 homes completed by 1968, but in 1983 they were demolished after the tenants complained about problems with damp, condensation and high heating costs.

Supermarket shopping was well established in the 1960s, but the prices have changed. This is Tesco's window on 3 September 1968.

Chief Constable of Leeds Mr James Angus, policewoman Christine Ingham (centre) and policewoman Rita Mogg are persuaded to take part in the publicity for the newly released film of *Chitty Chitty Bang Bang* on 25 November 1968.

The General Post Office in Leeds City Square. Designed by Sir Henry Tanner and completed in 1896, this building provided a striking first impression of the city for visitors arriving by train in October 1968. City Square was later redeveloped with the closure of a road that ran along the front of the Post Office building, and the Post Office building is now restaurants and apartments.

Leeds Head Post Office on 9 October 1968. Postcodes had not yet been introduced, and most letter sorting is carried out by hand by a team of workers.

Children's Day was a massive occasion, funded by the *Yorkshire Evening Post* and organised by local teachers. Pupils from just about every school in Leeds congregated in Roundhay Park arena for dancing, displays and sports. There was a Children's Day Queen and attendants, a fancy-dress parade and a bonny baby competition. On 8 July 1968 Mrs Ewart Clay, wife of the then editor of the *Yorkshire Evening Post*, crowned Amanda Merrikin, aged seven, as Queen of Children's Day in the arena.

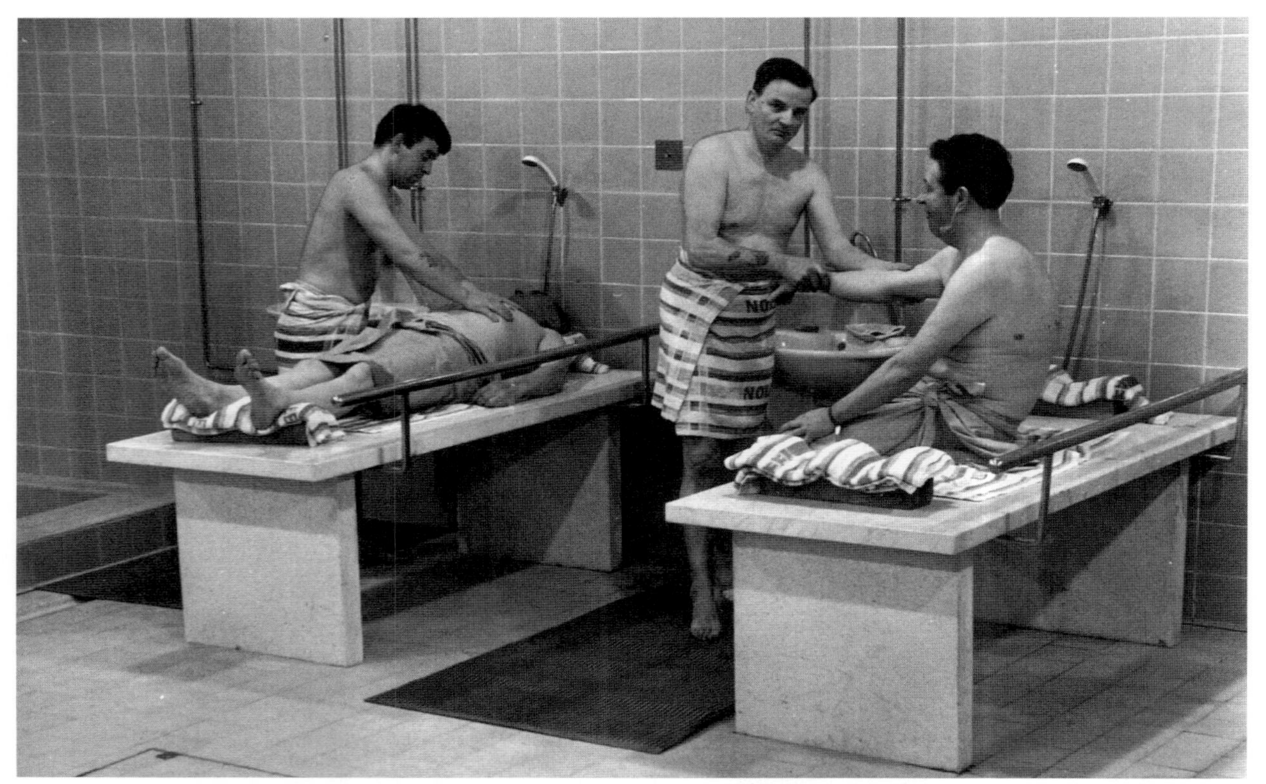

Although not an innovation in Leeds, Turkish Baths were available at the new Leeds International Pool, Westgate, pictured on 2 January 1968.

The Leeds tailoring trade employed thousands of workers before the war, but there were still many working in the trade in 1960s. This picture of women sewing is dated 16 May 1968 and was taken at David Little and Co. Ltd, Water Lane, Holbeck.

Bean Ings Mills, Wellington Street, Leeds. The mill dates from 1792 and was built by Benjamin Gott as the world's first woollen mill. The mill was demolished in the 1960s, and the *Yorkshire Evening Post* building now occupies the site. Wellington Bridge, Wellington Road, crosses the River Aire left of the mill.

Ancient loom.

The Great Synagogue in Belgrave Street, Leeds, on 7 October 1968. It was first opened in 1861.

This view of Bond Street, Leeds, is dated 8 August 1968 and shows the new office blocks under construction.

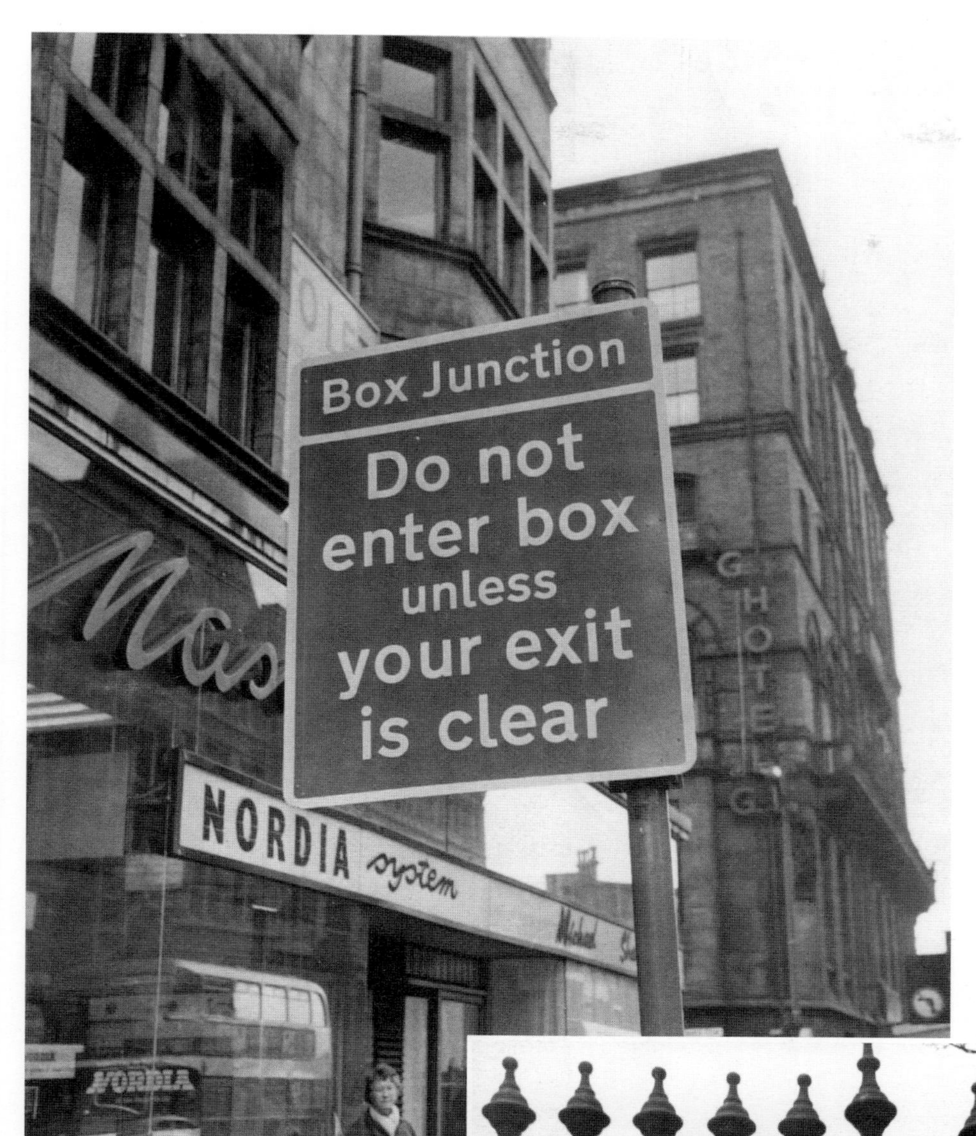

King Street, Leeds, 17 October 1968. A new sign appears at the junction of King Street and Wellington Street to try to stop traffic jams.

South Lodge in Holbeck, pictured here in 1968, was originally built as a Poor Law institution, often known as the 'workhouse'.

The former Leeds School of Medicine on Park Street on 22 June 1968.

Leeds Head Post Office, 14 October 1968.

Leeds Head Post Office, 14 October 1968.

Post Office, 23 July 1968. Mr Norman Petty by the nameplate in the little known Minor and Scurr's Yard, off Briggate.

Leeds Head Post Office, 19 September 1968. A challenge for the sorters.

Leeds Head Post Office, 18 December 1968. Mr Dennis Allison, one of the Post Office employees, is busy sorting through a mountain of damaged and undeliverable parcels in a Leeds storeroom.

24 February 1968. Mrs P. Faulconbridge demonstrates a Multilith 1250 systems machine. Multigraph Ltd and Admel International Ltd, Leeds.

Leeds Head Post Office, 14 October 1968.

Leeds Head Post Office, 14 October 1968.

Moortown, 8 May 1968. Cpl. Geoffrey Ridsdill (17), of Leafield Drive, Moortown, is pictured receiving his Queen's Award from Inspecting Officer Mr Roland Peck, Leeds Battalion President.

Belle Vue Civic Youth Club, 28 September 1968.

Two views of Leeds taken from Bishopgate Street looking towards City Square.

St James's Hospital, 1968. Work in progress on new extensions to the hospital in Beckett Street. The hospital was already one of the largest in Europe. In the foreground is all that remains of Museum Street, in a large area of old property which has been demolished.

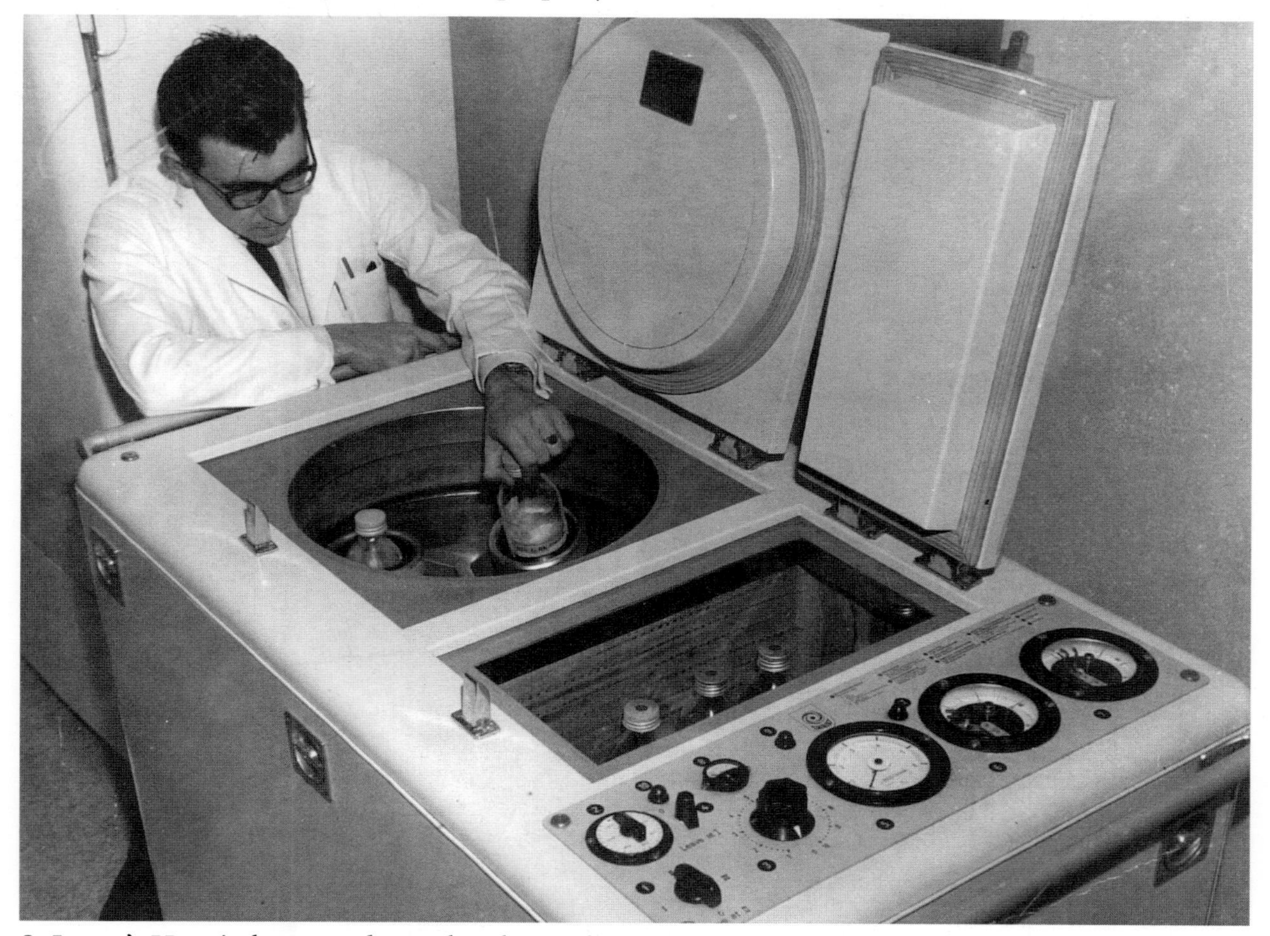

St James's Hospital, 1968. Plasma bottles are being put into the centrifuge machine.

A Headrow traffic island, 18 November 1968.

St Peter's Street between the Eastgate roundabout and the York Street traffic lights, photographed at 9.20am on 11 November 1968.

Hunslet Road traffic at the junction with Waterloo Road. The photograph was taken between 8.30 and 9am on 28 October 1968.

Chapeltown, 11 June 1968. The exterior of the Polish Catholic Centre in Newton Hill Road, Chapletown, showing the new extensions at each side of the building.

Leeds City Station, 1968.

Sandhurst Street, Calverley, 1968. View from the kitchen: Mrs Eileen Spencer surveys the mill wall opposite the window of her home.

Junction of the Headrow and Albion Street, 8 January 1968.

Briggate, 11 March 1968. Road-straddling traffic indicators.

Headrow, 19 October 1968.

Beeston, 5 April 1968. What remains of the nearest telephone box, Algeria Grove.

Boar Lane, 7 February 1968. Pedestrians dodge the traffic as they cross Boar Lane at the junction with City Square.

Hunslet, 20 February 1968. One of the lamps in Pearson Street, Hunslet, which is fed by North Sea gas.

Assembly Rooms, 16 October 1968.

Covered shelter in front of the Queens Hotel, City Square, Leeds 1968.

Armley Gaol, 15 January 1968. Part of the laundry.

Pudsey Library in the Town Hall, late 1960s.

Leeds's most famous statue, Edward the Black Prince, is having a clean-up by Stanley Briggs of the Leeds Corporation Works Department on 14 October 1969. The statue of the Black Prince was brought to City Square in Venetian style by barge from Hull along the Aire and Calder Navigation and unveiled on 16 September 1903.

The Herzl Moser Hospital in Leopold Street, Chapeltown, in 1969. Jews have lived in Leeds since about 1750, but the largest influx of Jews was after the pogroms of 1881 in Russia. Many initially lived in the Chapeltown area, where the Herzl Moser Hospital was set up in 1905.

This picture from 1969 was taken from the end of Rayner Drive, showing Farrar Lane and part of the land up to the GPO tower at Cookridge. It was taken just before work started on the Holt Village development.

The Queen's Hotel and Tatler Cinema in 1969. The Tatler Cinema was part of the Queen's Hotel building, next to the railway station. The cinema was opened as the News Theatre on 22 August 1938. It became the Classic in 1966, the Tatler Film Club in 1969 and reverted to the Classic in 1979. The building is Grade II listed.

Middleton Broom Colliery, Belle Isle, is demolished in May 1969. Middleton Broom, which closed in 1968, had been a large source of employment in the area. Middleton Park now occupies the site, separating Middleton from Belle Isle.

Vehicles outside Leeds Register Office, Park Square East, in December 1969. The parking meter was a recent addition to the Leeds scene.

Leeds Head Post Office, 14 July 1969. Parcels being sorted by hand at West Street Parcels Office, where the giant mechanical sorting machine has been halted by the Post Office engineers strike.

A postman empties a traditional postbox in Albion Place, Leeds, on 29 January 1969.

The new rectangular 'easier-to-empty' pillar postbox near the Westgate Circus, on 31 December 1969. Posting a letter is 16-year-old Angela Dunnhill of Taylor Grove, Methley.

Leeds Head Post Office, 11 August 1969.

Park Lane 20 February 1969. The 1,000th postbox of the Leeds Head Postmaster's area. It is of the new rectangular type.

Headrow, 17 November 1969. Stanley Munday's newspaper stand. The new-look *Sun* newspaper has not arrived.

On Street Lane, Roundhay, Mr Tom Lord (left), general manager of Leeds City Transport, and Ald. Col. Lawrence Turnbull, chairman of Leeds Transport and Trading Committee, inspect the first of 300 bus shelters which were being erected in Leeds by an advertising company in 1969.

Alwoodley bus shelter, 1969. Mr J.A. Kellis is pictured at the bus shelter at Alwoodley, rubbing his hands to keep warm.

Open-plan bus shelter at the junction of Dewsbury Road and the Ring Road, Beeston 1969.

St James's Hospital in 1969. The new out-patients and accident department is being built.

The pedestrian crossing across Park Row, near the junction of the Headrow, caused controversy in October 1969. The position of the crossing point meant that pedestrians had to take their lives in their hands to avoid traffic turning from the Headrow.

16 December 1969, Wortley. Mr Andrew Ross takes his daughter's baby for an outing down muddy Wheelwright Avenue, Lower Wortley. With him is two-year-old Colin Glacken, who lived in the avenue.

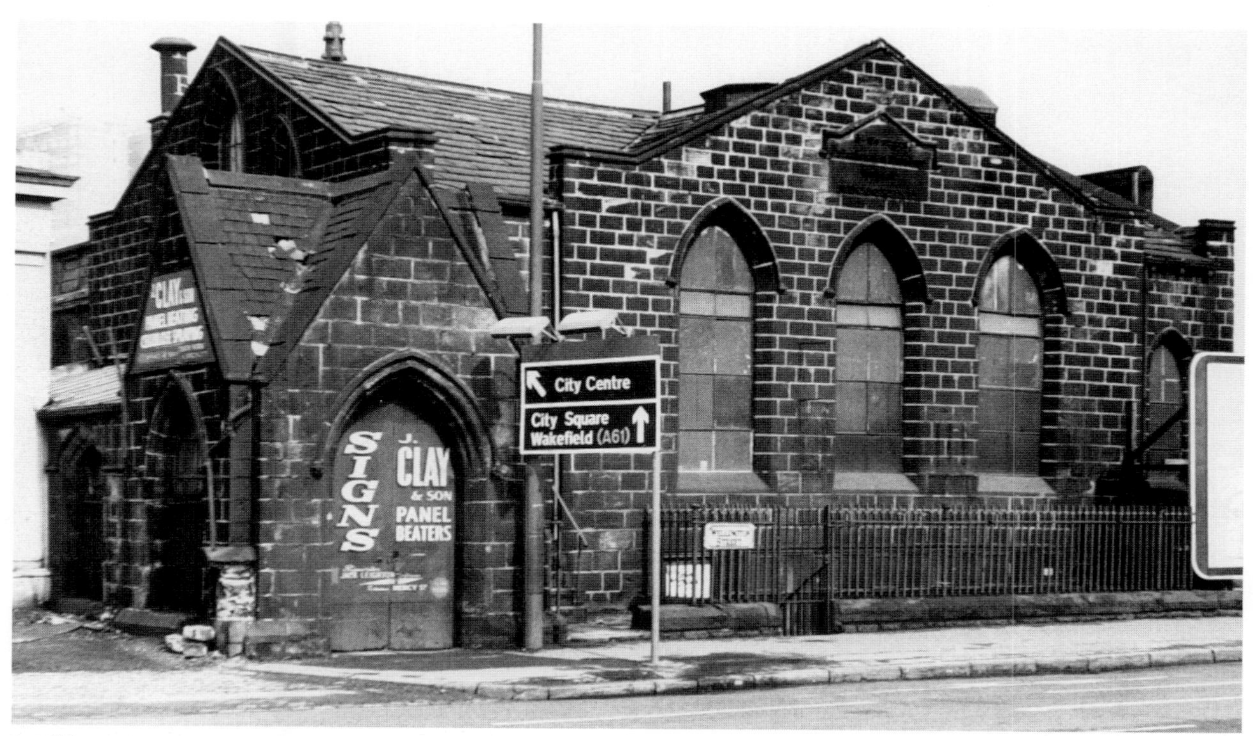

Wellington Street, Leeds, on 11 April 1969. The former St George's Sunday School Building, taken over by J. Clay & Son, panel beaters, was demolished soon after this picture was taken.

A familiar view today after almost 40 years. Traffic problems at Bridge End, Leeds, on 12 November 1969.

The former White Chapel, Hunslet Lane, was used by industrial firms when this picture was taken in 1969. At the right hand of the building is the old manse.

The residents of Sycamore Avenue, Halton, were divided over the fate of the sycamore trees, which lined the avenue in 1969.

The Hol Beck, from which the Holbeck district of Leeds derives its name, pictured from a bridge in Domestic Street in 1969.

The Black Prince statue in City Square, 16 August 1969.

Mr William McGreavey (left) and Mr Harry Haley cleaning the statue of the Black Prince in City Square, 19 September 1969.

The Odeon Cinema, opened 15 May 1969.

The Odeon cinema on the corner of New Briggate and the Headrow, 5 May 1969. Carl and Eve Foreman are pictured visiting Theatre 2 of the new Odeon Twin Theatres, which staged a gala performance of *Makenna's Gold* on 15 May, produced by Mr Foreman.

Tetley Hall, Headingley, Leeds, 10 January 1969. Mock supermarket setup by the Leeds Federation of Townswomen's Guilds as a practical illustration at their conference on decimal coinage. Examining the prices are (left to right), Mrs G. Maston, Mrs M. Dibb, Mrs P. Craven, Mrs E. Lumb, and Mrs S.M. Drayton.

Leeds Civic Hall's three telephone operators. Pictured with supervisor Mrs Cynthia Horn, they are (from front to back) Mrs Joy Davison, Miss Kathleen Hart and Mrs Virginia Wright. It is a new cordless exchange, pictured on 6 April 1969.

Leeds Public Dispensary, June 1969, isolated by work being carried out on the inner ring road schemes.

Armley Park, 29 August 1969. Mr Louis Fett, head gardener at Armley Park, with a floral design he has made to commemorate the centenary of the Amateur Swimming Association.

The Union Street Swimming Pool, near Millgarth in the centre of Leeds, in April 1969, shortly before its demolition.

The Junction, 6 August 1969.

The Fisherman's Hut, 11 August 1969.

Dark Arches Road in Leeds, 28 February 1969. It runs beneath the City Station towards Neville Street.

Children's Day Queen Suzanne Allman (7) of Montagu Crescent, Roundhay, 2 July 1969.

An advertisement from 1969.

Back New York Street, 26 October 1969. 'No litter' warnings and a vast amount of rubbish and litter.

Bishopgate Street, 7 November 1969. The junction of Neville Street and Dark Arches.

The precinct in Burley Lodge Road, 17 November 1969.

Chapel Allerton, 19 November 1969, shopping centre.

Chapel Allerton, 17 November 1969. The Yorkshire Bank Computer Centre.

Gipton Fire Station, 3 September 1969. A last-minute polish for fire-fighting equipment in preparation for a visit by the Lord Mayor Alderman A. R. Bretherick.

Blackman Lane, December 1969. There was controversy over the fate of this elm tree.

Merrion Centre, 11 December 1969. Christmas illuminations.

1970s

On 31 December 1970 Mr Tommy Dobson and Billy Boy make their way up a steep hill in the Little London area of Leeds.

Heavy traffic near Leeds city centre on 26 September 1970.

At St George's Crypt early arrivals stake their claim to bench space where they will spend the night. The crypt was founded by the vicar of St George's, the Revd Don Robbins, in the 1930s and has provided shelter for the city's homeless since then. It continues to provide services to over 130 homeless and disadvantaged people every day.

The Astoria Ballroom on Roundhay Road was opened as the Palais de Danse in 1929 and for 60 years was a popular venue. The dancing finished in 1992 and the building later became Amrik's electrical store and a gym, Fitness 2000. The site was sold for flats, and the much-loved building was demolished in the spring of 2006. This picture was taken on 4 July 1970.

In April 1970 Leeds United were in their glory days and reached the FA Cup Final. This picture shows fans queueing for tickets at the West Stand Ticket Office at Elland Road. However, Leeds United's quest for FA Cup glory ended in failure. They drew with Chelsea 2–2 after extra-time at Wembley but lost the replay 1–2, again after extra-time, at Old Trafford on 29 April.

The day after a blaze which destroyed a sports store in the heart of Leeds on 29 January 1970. About 50 pupils at a nearby school of music were evacuated as firemen fought the flames.

The Rolling Stones at Leeds University in 1971. Mick Jagger, Keith Richards, Mick Taylor and Charlie Watts.

Leeds, 26 May 1971. The woman is Woodbine Lizzie, a Leeds street character.

Paper boys and girls leaving Fred Gaines's shop in Crossgates for their newspaper rounds on 31 May 1971. They are (from the left) Terence McQueenie (15), David Wainwright (14), Diana Oldroyd (16) and Gillian Brammer (15).

The Lisbon Street dormitory at the Salvation Army Leeds hostel in 1971.

This picture was take on 15 January 1971. It shows the telephone switchboard staff at an office in Park Place, Leeds.

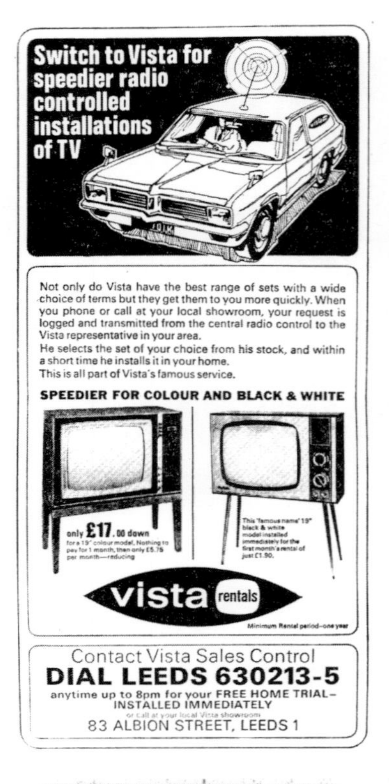

THERE'S A FOUR-FIGURE JACKPOT — ALWAYS!

A selection of advertisements from 1972.

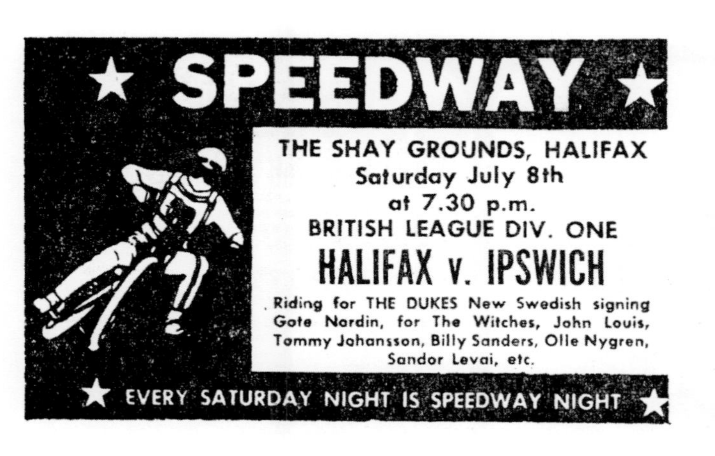

Inter'con'sort v.t.&i. To bring together, Keep company, Agree, Harmonise. (As in Intercon nightspots, q.v.)

intercon
the word's getting around

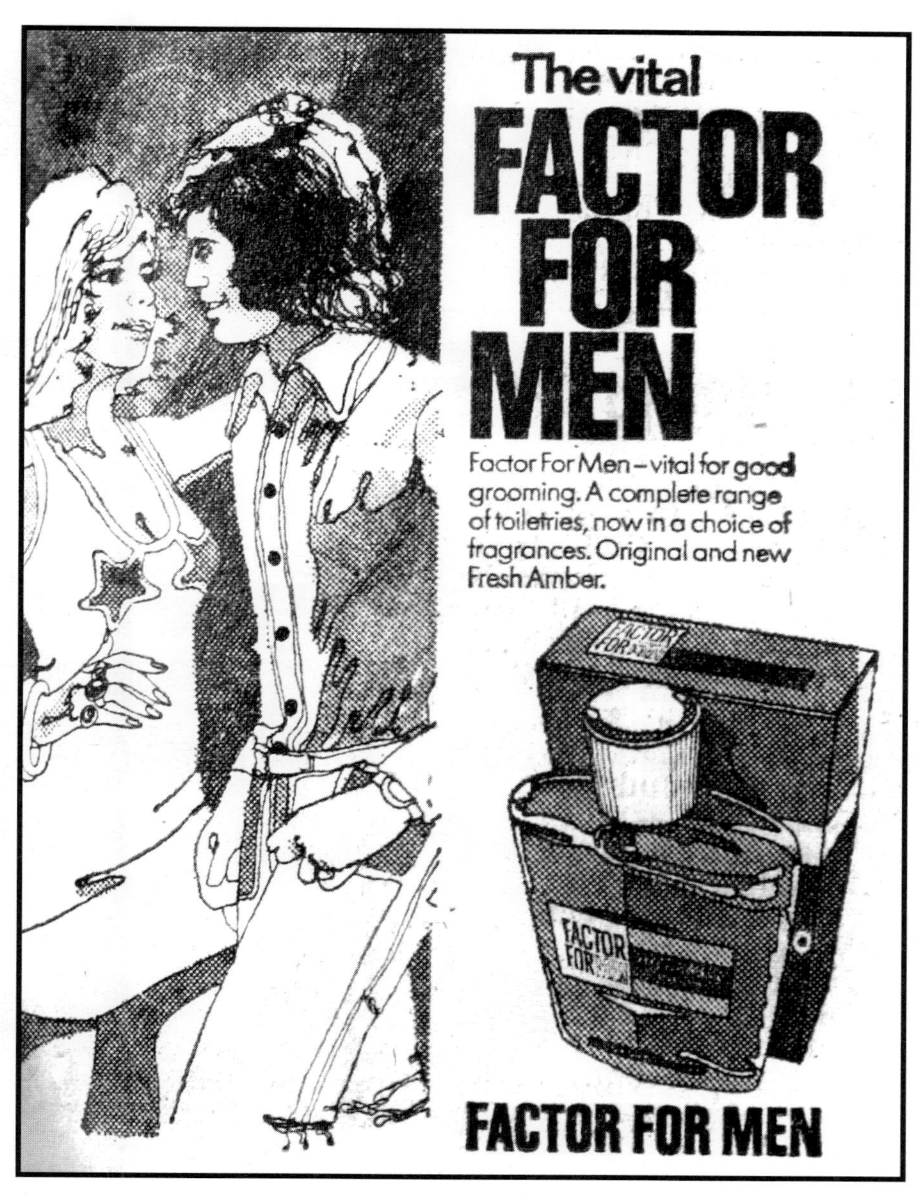

A selection of advertisements from 1972.

A Sheepskin in July?

Even this year a sheepskin seems a little extreme in July but when you can —

Buy Now and Save 20%

it's a wonderful investment for winter. A collection of this new season's styles that will be selling at normal prices (20% more) after July.

Offer Closes July 29th

Examples illustrated

YOUNG STYLE SHEEPSKIN
(Right)
With thong fastening and hood, attractive trimming at hood, front, hem and cuff. 35ins. long.
After July £55.00 —
£44.00
or £5.12 deposit and eight monthly payments of £5.15; total Hire Purchase price £46.32

THREEQUARTER JACKET
(Top left)
Cosy double breasted style in a wonderful new shade — vole.
After July £52.00 —
£41.60
or £4.62 deposit and eight monthly payments of £4.90; total Hire Purchase price **£43.82**

FASHION COAT
(Centre)
Full length with attractive braid fastening at front.
After July £93.50 —
£74.80
or £8.41 deposit and eight monthly payments of £8.80; total Hire Purchase price **£78.81**

RANCH SHEEPSKIN JACKET
(Lower left)
Very stylish and magnificent value.
After July £41.00 —
£32.80
or £3.75 deposit, and eight monthly payments of £3.85; total Hire Purchase price **£34.55**

FULL LENGTH SHEEPSKIN
(Not illustrated)
Single breasted style.
After July £53.00 —
£42.40
or £5.03 deposit and eight monthly payments of £4.95; total Hire Purchase price **£44.63**

Schofields

A selection of advertisements from 1972.

The £ is still worth a £ in the Isle of Man

The £ in your pocket still buys a full measure of holiday happiness in this holiday Island. Even in late August you'll find top-value, inclusive guest house accommodation from as little as £1.50 a day; or come in September and get the benefit of extra special budget tariffs!

Free golf on six superb courses during September! Unique Summerland entertainment centre gives guaranteed good weather for a huge range of holiday fun for all the family! Summer programme in full swing to mid-September, at eight fabulous resorts along 100 miles of beautiful, uncrowded coastline!

Act now to get full value out of Summer!

Send the coupon while the going's good.

To: Bond, Director of Tourism, Douglas, Isle of Man. Please send free colour brochure, accommodation and travel details to:

Name ____________________

Address ____________________

____

____

____

A selection of advertisements from 1972.

A selection of advertisements from 1972.

Commuters on their morning journey to Leeds on a winter's morning, 31 January 1972.

The Corn Exchange, 22 May 1972. Exterior picture showing the bars and shellfish bar.

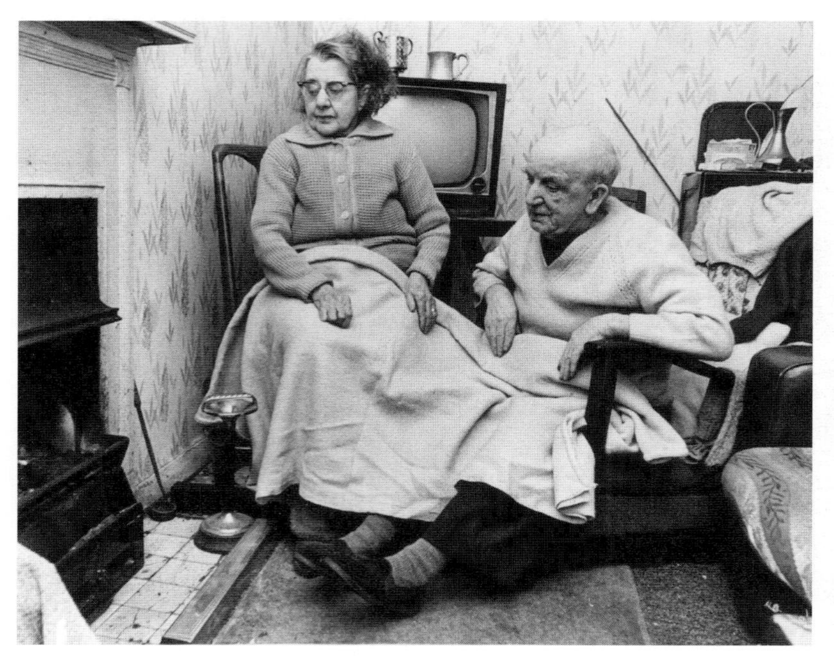

Leeds, Quarry Hill flats. Between 1938 and 1978 Quarry Hill was the largest social housing complex in the United Kingdom with radical features such as solid fuel ranges, electric lighting, a state-of-the-art refuse disposal system and communal facilities. However, due to poor construction methods and the general social problems with such developments the Quarry Hill flats were demolished in 1978. This picture, taken on 2 February 1972, shows William Creek, aged 77, and his wife Elsie, 74.

These pictures of Briggate show it in the 1970s. The picture above was taken on 16 September 1972. One of Leeds's oldest streets, its name comes from the Norse words for bridge and street. Private cars were banned from Briggate in 1973, and the street was pedestrianised in 1997.

The original meaning of Leeds Loiner is said to apply to someone born within the sound of the church bells in Briggate. Some 150 years ago there were many passages and yards leading to the backs of houses off Briggate, and these entries were known as 'Low Ins' which became 'Loins'. From this the term Leeds Loiner is said to derive. The other picture shows Briggate at night on 26 November 1975.

The arrival of Santa Claus at Leeds's department stores was a memorable event in many children's lives. On 4 December 1972 Father Christmas arrived at the Matthias Robinson store in Leeds aboard a veteran fire engine instead of a sledge. Matthias Robinson on Briggate opened in the 1890s but changed its name to Debenhams in 1972 soon after this picture was taken.

Danube Grove, off Gelderd Road, awaiting demolition in 1973.

On 20 September 1973 Hell's Angels rode into Leeds for the funeral of the president of the Leeds Chapter, Stephen Guest, who died in an incident in Derby. The 'Angels' acquired a fearsome reputation in the early days as wild young motorcyclists who dressed like pirates and wore Nazi emblems, but in Britain this was hardly ever justified, and they were really just unconventional people who dressed up and loved powerful motorcycles.

The 9ft-high gilded owls on top of the Civic Hall have looked over Leeds since 1933, although they have now been joined by four more. This picture was taken on 29 July 1973 and shows Kevin Maher of Clean Walls, Manchester, at work regilding the two owls.

Mr Cyril Hoffman beside the pumps at the filling station at Harehills, where customers were being rationed to a maximum of £1.50 worth of petrol in Britain's first oil price crisis, 27 November 1973.

A bride and bridegroom (on left), and five of the bridegroom's Teddy Boy friends, jive in Park Square Gardens on 2 February 1973 after a wedding at Leeds Register Office. The bridegroom was Mr Michael Shaw (20), second son of Mr and Mrs Ronald Shaw, Sissons Avenue, Middleton. The bride was Miss Sharman Dearlove, youngest daughter of Mr and Mrs Harry Dearlove, Helston Road, Middleton. The five friends are (left to right): Danny Gardner (17), Michael Allotey (18), Peter Shaw (18), Neil Higginbottom (16) and Graham Turner (17).

Holbeck in 1973.

The Leeds Mardi Gras carnival was first held in 1967 and was the first of its kind in Europe. This picture taken on 27 August 1973, in Chapeltown, shows Miss Movva Pinnock of Huddersfield, the carnival queen.

At the Bond Street precinct on 30 October 1974 comedians Morecambe and Wise make a personal appearance after they had appeared at Wakefield Theatre Club.

Boar Lane, 24 September 1974.

Heavy traffic during the morning rush into Leeds on a winter's morning, 24 January 1974.

The Bond Street shopping centre, later renamed Leeds Shopping Plaza, opened on 17 March 1977. This picture was taken on 29 November 1974.

The Bond Street shopping centre, later renamed Leeds Shopping Plaza, opened on 17 March 1977. This picture was taken on 23 June 1975 and shows the shopping centre under construction.

Traffic on the Headrow, which has acquired some new signs on 24 February 1975.

Newton Grove Post Office, Chapeltown Road, 2 April 1975.

Kirkstall Road on 3 March 1975.

On Saturday 13 December 1975 two-thirds of Kirkgate market was destroyed by fire. The cause of the fire is uncertain – some people said it was an electrical fault, others an overturned paraffin heater. Stallholders attempted to put out the fire, but it spread so quickly that they had to run for their lives. The smoke and flames could be seen from 15 miles away.

More than 100 firemen with 15 pumps and 221 jets fought the blaze, but before they could bring it under control most of the roof of the market had collapsed. Miraculously, everyone managed to leave the building and there were no casualties. The fire caused £7 million-worth of damage.

The 1904 market hall and the top section of the market were undamaged and were open for business again within three days. Traders who had lost their stalls were accommodated in other parts of the city. The site was cleared, and by July 1976 a new hall had been built and was ready for the traders to move in. A second hall opened in 1981. This photograph looks north across the wreckage.

The cricket World Cup came to Headingley on 18 June 1975 when England (95 all out) were beaten by Australia (96 for 6). Gary Gilmour took six England wickets for 14 runs and rescued the Australians with 28 after they were 39 for 6. John Driver (14) and Neil Anderton (16) of Silsden, were first in the queue at the juniors gate. First to arrive at the ground was Mr Nicholas Bush (25).

It is 21 June 1975 and the queues are outside at Lewis's store in the Headrow, as people wait for the doors to open for the start of the sale. Lewis's opened on 17 September 1932 as a store that had a greater variety of goods than any other in Leeds. Over 100,000 people visited the store on that first day. By the 1980s the firm was in trouble, and despite attempts to modernise the Leeds store (the ground floor was refurbished in 1984), the store closed in 1991 and the firm went into receivership. It was taken over by Owen and Owen of Liverpool in March 1991. In 1996 Owen and Owen stores were bought by Allders, but the much-loved store eventually closed. A redevelopment of the site into the Broad Gate centre of shops and offices has now taken place.

The Tower Picture House, pictured in 1975, opened in 1920 and became part of the Leeds-based Associated Tower Cinemas group. It was part of the frontage of the Grand Arcade on New Briggate and, when this picture was taken in 1975, had a rather ugly name board. The cinema closed in 1985.

The Leeds Society for Deaf and Blind People was formed in 1866 and for many years was based in Albion Street, on the site which later became Dudley House and the K apartments. It bought the former Leeds Public Dispensary, renaming it Centenary House, in 1976 and this picture, taken on 28 September 1976, shows some of the leisure facilities, including three full-size billiard tables.

A burning tyre dump on Pontefract Lane, Cross Green, sends a pall of smoke across the city on 9 February 1976.

It was 1977, and the troubles in Northern Ireland were continuing. In Vicar Lane, the Army's robot device for dealing with terrorist bombs was called in after a bomb scare. This picture, taken on 10 February 1977, shows the device, which was equipped with closed-circuit TV, being put back into its trailer after the bomb scare in Vicar Lane, Leeds.

Cross Gates, December 1977. The view from Tranquillity Walk looking across Austhorpe Road towards the National Westminster Bank.

Holbeck, 11 November 1977. Pickets from the fire brigade's union at Holbeck Police Station during the firemen's strike of that year. The army has stationed two fire tenders.

A selection of advertisements from 1978.

A selection of advertisements from 1978.

Traffic on Eastgate at 9am on 24 May 1978.

Pickets on Dewsbury Road during the Leeds City busmen's strike on 28 April 1978.

In the Merrion Centre in 1978 businessmen enjoy their lunch in pleasant surroundings.

The singing roadsweeper William Stockdale, 'Billy' to his many friends, brightened many a cold day for the people of Armley during the 17 years he had spent in the district, doing the rounds with his brush and cart. He is pictured serenading shoppers Mrs Daisy Illingworth (left) and Mrs Eva Mitchell in Agley on 25 January 1979.

York Road, 15 February 1979.

Holbeck, 29 April 1979. The postman is delivering on this cobbled street.

Leonards Store, Cross Gates, 1979.

Domestic Street, Holbeck, on 30 October 1979. Beatrice and Arthur Butt's corner shop.